MW01062158

ARIEL BOOKS

**Andrews McMeel
Publishing**

Kansas City

Blessings for Cats

Amy Hunt

Illustrated by Marian Nixon

In memory of:
Candy, Rusty 1, Rusty 2 (Lollypop), Peppermint, Caramel,
and Mama Cat with her white & tabby babies.
And for my blessed Chocolate Drop, who inspired me
with each word that I wrote!

Illustrations © 2005 by Marian Nixon
Book design by Maura Fadden Rosenthal / Mspace

ISBN-13: 978-0-7407-4160-9
ISBN-10: 0-7407-4160-8
Library of Congress Control Number: 2005921792

Introduction

Ever since felines were worshiped as deities in ancient Egypt thousands of years ago, mankind has been enjoying the companionship of cats. Their beauty, their capricious ways, and their whimsical natures are a source of endless fascination to those of us whose lives have been graced by their presence. We take part in their endearing playfulness one minute and stand back to admire their almost regal refinement and elegance the next.

Sometimes, as you will read, cats expand our lives with good fortune, incredible rescues, and amazing miracles. But most of the time we are content simply to enjoy the companionship and the ethereal sense of peace and pleasure that cats bring to us. Simply put, cats are blessings in our lives. This book celebrates and pays tribute to cats by offering them our heartfelt blessings in words of love, admiration, and appreciation for all that they do.

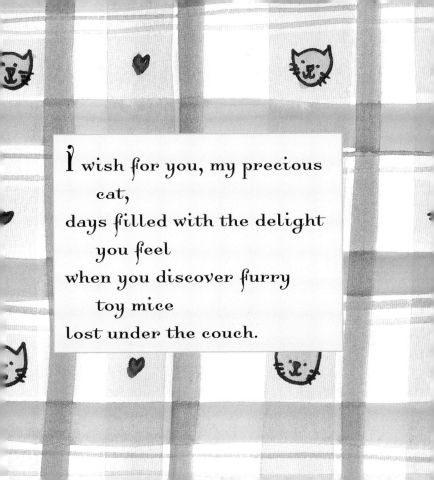

I wish for you, my precious cat,
days filled with the delight you feel
when you discover furry toy mice
lost under the couch.

I bless your wisdom
for knowing
when I need you and
for knowing
when I don't.

Bless you
  for each and every
laugh and smile
    you have ever given me.

Bless you for sharing
   your food with the dog
and ignoring the fact
   that he ate more of it
than you did.

Blessings on
     your beautiful mane of fur,
except when it's on
     my new black party dress!

Bless you
for gently reminding
me of my past feline loves,
while remaining
uniquely yourself.

I AM COMFORTED TO KNOW THAT THERE IS NO NEED TO UTTER MY PAIN OR JOY OUT LOUD, BECAUSE YOU, MY INTUITIVE FELINE, PROVE YOU UNDERSTAND UNSPOKEN WORDS WHEN YOU PURR AS YOU LIE IN MY LAP.

May you only play
with ponytail holders
when they are out of my hair!

Snowball Saves the Day

Snowball was an ordinary cat. At least that's what Jay and Susan Martin believed when they adopted him from the local animal shelter.

Snowball lived happily with the Martins for several years. In time, the Martins had their first child. When they brought baby Claire home from the hospital, they were happily surprised to find that Snowball reacted to the baby with a surprising protectiveness. He was never far from Susan's side when she cared for Claire.

One day when Claire was four months old, Susan put the baby down for her nap and went downstairs. She was careful to take the baby monitor with her so that she would know if Claire awoke. About fifteen minutes later, Snowball ran to Susan and began to meow loudly, trying to jump up on her. Susan scolded Snowball, but he didn't stop his strange behavior. Finally he left, but moments later Susan heard an odd moaning meow from the monitor. Susan rushed upstairs and hurried into the baby's room to find Snowball at the edge of the crib. When she hurried forward to quiet him, she saw that the baby was an odd bluish color and was very still. Grabbing Claire up, Susan ran to the phone and called 911.

Thanks to Snowball, Claire was rushed to the hospital, treated for a breathing ailment, and made a full recovery. Had Snowball not alerted Susan when he did, Claire would not have survived. Snowball proved to be a true blessing for the Martin family!

Your all-consuming joy over simple treats and toys gladdens my heart.

BEFORE YOU EVER CAME
INTO MY LIFE, I MISSED YOU.

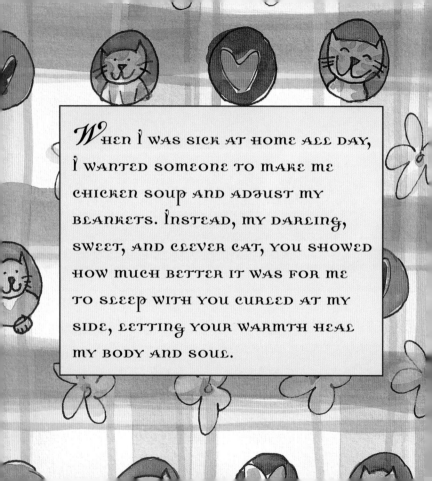

When I was sick at home all day, I wanted someone to make me chicken soup and adjust my blankets. Instead, my darling, sweet, and clever cat, you showed how much better it was for me to sleep with you curled at my side, letting your warmth heal my body and soul.

I PROMISE TO ALWAYS DO
MY BEST TO TAKE GOOD CARE
OF YOU.

Bless the invention of lint-off rollers— they help me love you more!

Bless you
for coming
when I call your name—
most of the time!

Bless you, my furry
feline—
may you always have a
soft, warm bed,
furry toys to play with,
a filled food dish,
and an open toilet.

Bless you for being an alarm
    clock
that doesn't need batteries
    and still comes with a
snooze alarm.

Bless you
    for listening
to me
        unconditionally.

I LOVE THE WAY YOU LOVE BEING SILLY. YOUR ANTICS MAKE ME LAUGH LONG AFTER THE INCIDENTS ARE OVER.

The Cat from Imado

A woman who lived in Imado, in the eastern part of Tokyo, had a pet cat that she cherished dearly. However, she was very poor, and one day she realized that she didn't have enough money to take care of him. Broken-hearted, she had to tell her dear friend that she would have to leave him on his own.

That very night, the old women had a dream in which her cat spoke to her, saying, "If you fashion my image in clay, it will bring you much luck."

The old woman listened to her dream and made the image of her cat into clay. Soon after, a guest came to visit. The guest liked the sculpture of her cat so much that he asked to buy it. From then on, the

old woman created many objects in her cat's like-
ness. Before long, she was blessed with considerable
wealth from selling her art. However, her truest
blessing was the fact that she had enough money to
provide for her treasured feline for all his days.

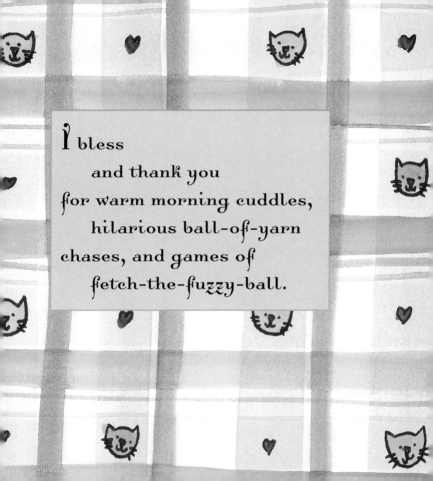

I bless
    and thank you
for warm morning cuddles,
    hilarious ball-of-yarn
chases, and games of
    fetch-the-fuzzy-ball.

May you always be
the first one to greet
me when I wake up
in the morning
and the last one
to send me off to bed
at night!

I CAN SAFELY SAY THAT WE ARE BOTH THANKFUL WHEN THE GROCERY STORE GIVES OUT PAPER BAGS INSTEAD OF PLASTIC. YOU HAVE YOUR FUN, AND I GET MINE FROM WATCHING YOU!

Bless you
    for not holding
it against me
    when I take you
to the vet.

I AM BLESSED TO LOVE YOU MORE THAN YOU LOVE NAPPING ON THE WINDOW SEAT.

Bless you
   for always
loving me
      despite my faults.

Bless you
    for being beautiful,
inside and out!

I NEVER TRULY UNDERSTOOD
THE CONCEPT OF THE SIXTH SENSE
UNTIL YOU GRACED MY LIFE.

Bless your unfailing hope
when you come running
anytime a can is opened,
food or otherwise!

May you always keep
your kind and
gentle heart.

May you always
keep
your sense of humor!

Bless you
    for letting the children
dress you up like a dolly.
    I promise you a treat
if you don't shake off
    the bonnet again!

Cat Fugue

$\mathcal{D}$omenico Scarlatti, an Italian composer who lived in the late seventeenth and early eighteenth centuries, captured the six random notes created as his cat walked across the keys of his harpsichord and used them as a theme for his work "The Cat Fugue." Throughout the piece, the odd combination of sharp, average, and subdued notes are repeated, as if the cat were continuing to saunter across the harpsichord.

Another famous account explains the origin of a Frédéric Chopin composition. It happened that while composing a waltz in F-major, Chopin artistically incorporated all the notes his cat performed as it ran across the piano keys. Chopin did not generally title his works, but this particular piece is often referred to as "The Cat Waltz."

For Scarlatti and Chopin, the cat was truly a blessed inspiration!

Bless you
for persuading me
to play with you
even when I'm tired.

WHEN I FINALLY GOT THAT NEW CD PLAYER I HAD BEEN SAVING UP FOR, MY FIRST THOUGHT WAS ABOUT ALL THE FUN YOU WOULD HAVE PLAYING WITH THE BOX IT CAME IN.

Bless you
    for not being offended
when one of my friends is
    allergic to you.

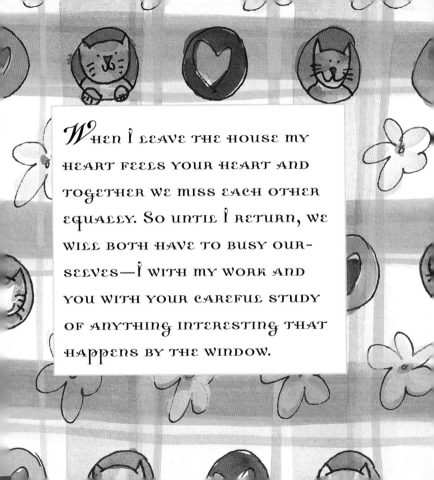

WHEN I LEAVE THE HOUSE MY HEART FEELS YOUR HEART AND TOGETHER WE MISS EACH OTHER EQUALLY. SO UNTIL I RETURN, WE WILL BOTH HAVE TO BUSY OUR-SELVES—I WITH MY WORK AND YOU WITH YOUR CAREFUL STUDY OF ANYTHING INTERESTING THAT HAPPENS BY THE WINDOW.

May you always
speak the same
language of love
as I do.

Bless you
    for always
letting me
    pick the movies to
watch on TV!

Bless you
    for knowing
that when certain people
    come to visit us,
you can't climb
    all over them.

In the olden days, people warmed bricks in the fire, wrapped them in towels, and placed them at the end of their bed to warm their feet. I am blessed to have you instead!

Bless you
for accepting
those times when
I don't understand
your specific meows.

Bless you
    for always
listening to me—
    and never talking my
ear off in return.

Dandelion

The Sandersons, who lived near Chicago, Illinois, had a black, yellow, and orange striped tabby called Dandelion. One spring, Mr. Sanderson was unexpectedly offered a temporary job in California. The family decided that since they would only be leaving their home in Illinois for six months, they would leave Dandelion with their grandparents, who lived about three hundred miles away on a farm in northern Wisconsin. The grandparents were fond of cats and could offer Dandelion what seemed liked the perfect temporary home.

A month after the Sandersons moved to California, they received a distressing phone call from Wisconsin.

Dandelion had been missing for almost two weeks! At first the grandparents thought she was just out exploring. However, with each passing day they were convinced that some unfortunate fate had come to her. Naturally, the family was heartbroken.

Months passed with no sign of Dandelion. The Sandersons returned to Illinois. After they had been home for more than six months, they were absolutely astounded to find a filthy, exhausted, and bleeding cat at their door. Dandelion had returned home! It had taken her nearly twelve months to find her way. The Sandersons could only imagine what she must have endured during her journey of three hundred miles.

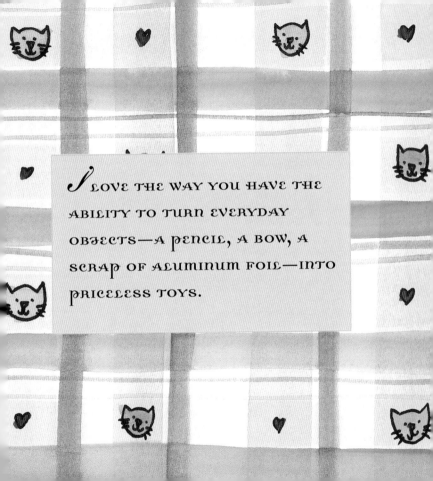

I LOVE THE WAY YOU HAVE THE ABILITY TO TURN EVERYDAY OBJECTS—A PENCIL, A BOW, A SCRAP OF ALUMINUM FOIL—INTO PRICELESS TOYS.

Bless you
    for making me
feel special
    whether I give you
a treat or not!

Bless you
for letting me
be in a bad mood
and loving me
regardless.

Bless you
    for sometimes pretending
you are human.

Bless you
    for sometimes pretending
I am a cat.

Bless you
    for having nine lives
and for sharing one of them
    with me!